Of Little Faith: A Psychologically & Faith-Based Journey Through Anxiety

Carmelita Booker

ISBN: 1539464113
ISBN-13: 978-1539464112

DEDICATION

To anyone who has anxiety or depression and needs to know that they are not alone. And to the Savior who said, "to everyone who has been given much, much will be demanded; and from the one who has been entrusted with much, much more will be asked." Luke 12:17

CONTENTS

ACKNOWLEDGMENTS

I give a special thank you to Dr. Meyer and Dr. Lebovits who have supported me and continue to professionally mold me. And a thank you to my dad, Gary Booker who has encouraged me to write since I first learned how.

CHAPTER 1: THE BEGINNING

I grew up in Chicago, or as pop culture refers to it, "Chiraqu" although it didn't feel like Chiraqu to me. I had a pretty normal childhood, I liked to play outside and grow things with my dad and neighbor and I played in the park and ran around in our huge yard. I guess there was gang violence but I never noticed. My mom told me that when I was a baby she took me to the park and gangs started shooting at each other so he had to run home with me, dodging bullets all the way back. I don't remember that though, I remember summertime in Chicago being the best thing ever. I don't remember ever being bothered by the things that bother me now; like mosquitos, the itchiness the humidity brings, the heat. I loved the heat, I don't think I got many mosquito bites until I moved to the suburbs, and I don't remember it ever being humid. I remember the ice cream carts, not trucks, carts. There were men that came around with ice cream cars, corn carts, and watermelon carts. It was amazing. I loved summer; I loved it not only because it was a break from everything. Growing up in Chicago meant something different to my parents than it did to me at the time. My parents put me into private school because of the violence at Chicago Public Schools. I think they thought it would be safer and they were right, however Chicago private schools were no walk in the park either. I think the first time I experienced racism was when I was in kindergarten. Yes, I was five. I didn't understand all the insults at the time, but as I grew older I understood. The first time I experienced racism was when I was walking down the stairs so that I could go outside to meet my carpool group. I was walking behind 6th graders and for some reason they turned around and started yelling at me, they told me I was slow, yelled racial and sexist slurs, and called me names in Spanish. You see, most of the people I went to school with were Hispanic. There were few white people and even fewer black people. The racism wasn't all that bad though, there were some funny moments; like the time one kid asked me if I was black because I drank too

3

much chocolate milk. He was dumbfounded when I told him I was lactose intolerant and hated chocolate. By the time I was in the 2nd grade I loathed school. It was exhausting. It felt like I never got a break, if it wasn't an upperclassman it was someone in my class heckling at me, "Your dad's poor," "You live in a box," "You're ugly." After my parents talking to the principal and an 8th grader getting suspended for bullying me, after me going to the teachers repeatedly and nothing being done, after being humiliated too many times to count, I decided to take matters into my own hands. I had to get tough, I didn't have a choice. I wasn't good with words; I was really quiet so I used everything but words to fight. One time, a kid called me a clown so I bit him. Another time a girl called my cousin "loca," so I slapped her around a few times. I was a fighter and I was angry all the time. It got to the point where no one bothered me but a couple of upperclassmen that I knew I couldn't fight. The teachers always told my parents and my parents didn't care, they knew that school was hell for me and they knew that the teachers did nothing. Essentially, I was taught to fight back.

When I was ten we moved to the northwest suburbs of Chicago and I was not thrilled. Everything was different, there were no ice cream carts, no watermelon carts, no corn carts…we had to go to the store for our popsicles now and make our own corn. Summer was okay, I made some friends in my neighborhood and we rode bikes, which was weird for me because in Chicago I had only ever roller bladed. But no one roller blades in my suburbs, they ride bikes or jog. It was hard for me to sleep the first couple of weeks in our new home because in Chicago I always went to sleep to the sound of police sirens and cars zooming by. In the suburbs there was hardly a car that drove by the house at night, there were only the sounds of trains, bugs, and animals. I remember the first time I heard the train go by, my whole room was shaking so I thought we were having an earthquake, I hid under the covers because I didn't know what to do in the event of an earthquake, I guess I thought the covers would protect me. Real culture shock didn't happen to me until school started, though. I sat at the front of the class and looked around at all the students, and witnessed two things that were so rare to me: everyone was nice to me, *everyone* and no one spoke any Spanish, *at all*. Keep in mind I was ten, so I thought every pale skinned person spoke Spanish. Because I knew so many Mexicans, Puerto Ricans, and Cubans in Chicago, and because so many of the Puerto Ricans had pale skin, I assumed most pale skinned people were Hispanic. To my surprise, that wasn't at all true. Everyone in my class was white and they didn't seem to care that I was black. It was crazy to me. I made friends so easily, it was effortless. I was still a quiet person but my goofiness seemed to attract people. However, by the time 6th grade rolled around my teacher and the school social worker were concerned with my social standing. They said that with middle school around the corner and then high school they were concerned that I would have a hard time making friends, so they made me skip English class to meet with the social worker a couple of times a week. The social worker told me I could invite friends if I wanted. So of course, I invited people! What twelve-year-old doesn't want to skip class? I invited my closest friends, who invited other friends, who invited more friends. We all sat around her table waiting for her to come through the door. I didn't understand it at the time, but when she opened the door her eyes widened. She asked me to introduce her to everyone so I did. She asked us about what was going on in our lives and we started talking about this mean girl we didn't like. The social worker asked why people put up with her if she's mean. One of the girls blurted out, "because she's popular!" The social worker then asked us if we thought we needed to be mean in order to be popular. The same girl blurted, "well no, Carmelita is popular and she's the nicest girl in school!" I think I was more dumbfounded than the social worker at this point. The social worker looked at me and asked if I thought I was popular and I laughed and said no. To me popular was the pretty girl who was loud and obnoxious and attention grabby. Popular was the girl everyone wanted to look like. No one wanted to look like me. And I was far from loud and even farther from attention grabby. The other girls quickly chimed in and said, "you know everyone from the other classes," "everyone likes you," "you're sweet," "you're cool." This was a complete 180 from what I had experienced in Chicago. *Popular. Me.* I didn't get it, all I was doing was being a goof ball and being nice to most people. I had sleepovers at my house a couple of times a month and people came, people wanted to sit with me at lunch. I was never lonely; I was never alone.

CHAPTER 2: HOW TO [PRETEND TO] BE BRILLIANT

High school was normal, basically normal. It wasn't until college that my life got interesting again. I stumbled through my undergraduate career. I was by no means a great student, I tried but I wasn't that good at anything it seemed. I was an education major for a year and got bored so I switched to pre-nursing but I wasn't good at the "hard" sciences like microbiology, they were a lot of fun but I wasn't good at memorizing terms and definitions and photos. So I changed my major to psychology. I still struggled with some courses but for the most part I enjoyed it. My senior year rolled around and I had a meeting with one of my professors. I wanted to go to graduate school but I didn't know what to specialize in. I told her I was interested in cognitive psychology but I was also interested in children and adolescent psychology and I noticed that I had a knack for industrial and organizational psychology. She bluntly told me that she did think I was competitive enough for cognitive psychology. I appreciated her candidness, it was one of the reasons I admired her and I knew she was right, my grades did not measure up to the other students who would be applying to the cognitive psychology programs. Still I was angry, I wanted to know *how* I could be a competitor, not that I wasn't, I already knew I wasn't. I graduated with a 2.33 and I was just happy to be out of school. After college I struggled to find a job, like most college graduates. I was a daycare teacher part-time while I looked for something better. All the while what my professor said still stuck in my brain like gum on rug; I couldn't get it out of my head, *you're not competitive enough, and I'm not saying this to be mean I'm just explaining the reality.* I really wanted to try to be competitive. I sought out internships in psychology, anything I could find and eventually I landed an internship that I was underqualified for…on paper. It was an internship with these psychologists who had come up with self-help therapeutic techniques for battling anxiety, tunnel vision effect, and impulsiveness. The intern they were looking for in their description had to have a very high GPA, I don't remember what it was exactly, I only remember that mine was far from it. The intern also had to have knowledge, skills, and abilities that I believed I had or could adapt to quickly. I applied not expecting to even get a phone interview. A couple of weeks went by and I received an e-mail requesting a phone interview. I called the psychologist after church and many words were exchanged and the interview was going very well. But then he asked me what my GPA was. I told him reluctantly that it was a two-point-something, I honestly couldn't remember what. He said something along the lines of, "well I will be honest with you, we only take brilliant students so here is your chance to convince me you are brilliant." I immediately got nervous, *I'm not brilliant,* I thought. And immediately after that I thought to myself, *I don't have to believe I'm brilliant, I just have to make him believe I am.* So I decided to spare him the sob story about how my GPA was a three-point-something until I transferred schools and got sick and my grandma died, realistically everyone has a reason for a low GPA, that's not what he was asking for. Instead I told him my goals. The internship was for curriculum writing so I told him about how one of my long term goals is to develop curricula for students in impoverished schools and non-profits in the US and abroad. I told him that I wanted to go to graduate school in order to achieve this goal. And I told him that I found the brain fascinating and that I was very aware of how people perceive me on paper, I was aware that I was not a stand out candidate and I talked about how I didn't care about what they thought. I told him that I wouldn't let my past obstacles interfere with my goals and that I wanted to be in a position to help students like myself. When I was done trying to convince him that I'm brilliant, he told me that after talking to me he had no doubt that I would be a great intern. He said that he felt that my GPA wasn't a good reflection of my intelligence and that he would be happy to work with me and, if all went well, write me a letter of recommendation for graduate school. Shortly after that, I applied to graduate school and after an interview that went similarly to the one above, I received a welcome letter. I had been accepted into an industrial and organizational psychology Master's program.

CHAPTER 3: WHEN I GROW UP

After about six months I landed a job at a hospital as a registrar. For those of you who don't know what a registrar is, it's basically a person who verifies insurance. I worked in the ER most of the time and I was on second shift, I was good at it but I wasn't happy. The hospital was in a period of transition so I had to learn how to use new software right after my initial training and after having worked with the old software for three months. I continued with my internship and my classes because both were online so that allowed me to have a full-time work schedule. Working at the hospital was very hard on my self-esteem because it wasn't a job that required a college degree, it was as if all those years in school and everything I went through was for nothing. Some mornings I would wake up and grab my diploma just to read it and remind myself I graduated college. Most of the people I worked with didn't have a Bachelor's and some were in school or thinking of going back. At the same time though it was inspiring because I was surrounded by people who wanted to better themselves. I met physician assistants with dreams of turning the hospital into a tech-savvy environment. I met nurses who were going back to school to be nurse practitioners. I met technicians who were working full time, supporting their families, and going back to school to be nurses. All around me was inspiration and it kept my dreams alive as well. I became increasingly interested in neurology and decided to meet with the neuropsychologist on staff. I walked into her office and butchered her name as I talked to the registrar in her office, she corrected me a couple of times and told me to have a seat. While I waited for her I looked around and tried to picture what my practice would look like, would I have cheesy posters on the wall? Would there be toys for children to play with, would I specialize in pediatrics or geriatrics? Even if I don't specialize in pediatrics should I still have toys?

She came through the door and called my name. She was not at all what I expected. She was young, tall, and beautiful. She walked through the door with this gorgeous dress suit that was clearly designer and heels that were business-chic. She was friendly and open and allowed me to sit in on a case. She walked me through what she does on a daily bases and I asked her if she had any research interests. She told me that she was interested in Alzheimer's disease and that she was writing a book as well. Near the end of my visit I thought, *this woman is amazing, she's a practicing psychologist and a*

8

researcher, she writes books and she goes to conferences. She is what I want to be when I grow up! I looked around her office inspired with stars in my eyes and read her degrees. I had already done background research on her before my visit so I knew where she studied, interned and fellowshipped. But suddenly, looking at her degrees first-hand it hit me. I would never study at UW Milwaukee, one of the top psychology research institutions in the country. And I could never perform my internship at Yale and land a fellowship at Harvard Medical School. *You're not competitive enough,* I said to myself as I tried to put my life in perspective to my dreams. When my visit was over I told her I saw myself as more of a pediatric neuropsychologist, mostly because I wanted to get out of there before I had an anxiety attack. I politely thanked her, she gave me her business card and told me to stay in touch, she seemed more excited about my future than I was.

CHAPTER 4 AN [IM]POSSIBLE FUTURE

I wanted to end my internship. The psychologist I had been working with sent me a text about a project he wanted me to work on and I told him I was just too busy with school and work; I was always tired. He told me that had I told him that I felt overworked, he would have lightened my load and let me work part-time. He continued on saying that I fall into a trend where I assume the worst, expect the worst, and prepare for the worst. And I thought to myself, *maybe that's because the worst is always happening.* But I didn't say anything. He pointed me to a previous conversation I had with his business partner, he was a psychologist too. I called his partner because I was having a hard time deciding what graduate school to go to for my Master's degree and what to specialize in. But that wasn't the real problem. The real problem was that I was doubting my steps. Did I have what it takes to be a graduate student? What if I choose the wrong program? What if it doesn't matter what program I choose because I'll fail regardless? And even if I graduate, what if I can't don't get into a doctoral program and I just dug myself a deeper debt hole? I knew my undergraduate grades were not competitive enough for a doctoral program right off the bat so my plan was to get a Master's degree first so that I could prove to admissions committees that I could handle graduate coursework. My fear was that I would apply to these Master's programs and get rejected, resorting to having to apply to some school that accepts everyone and thus lessening my chances of getting into a solid doctoral program. My fear of rejection came true after getting my first rejection letter. And then my fear solidified after receiving my second rejection letter. *Should I even bother?* During my phone conversation I expressed all of these fears. He asked me to imagine what would happen if things go right. I was puzzled and asked him what he meant. He told me to picture myself in a dark room opening a door and through that door I saw everything I've wanted. I didn't understand how this would help me. I felt that it would drive me deeper into depression because I would be envisioning an impossible future that I wanted but couldn't have. He told me to do it anyway and e-mail him my thoughts. So I thought about it. I walked through a door and I saw myself as a psychologist who was active in research and clinical practice. I saw myself traveling to different countries to help implement curricula I wrote. I saw myself working with inner city schools in the US to implement curricula I wrote. I saw myself consulting for firms and I saw myself happy. Although I still wasn't sure any of it was possible.

CHAPTER 5: THE ATTACKS

I can't do this.

I kept panting and telling myself over and over and over again, *I can't do this.*

I kept repeating it between gasps of and sobs, *I can't do this, I can't, I can't…do this, I can't…*My roommate was gone for the night because it was a Friday night so I knew I wouldn't see her until the next day…or 3 in the morning. So I knew it was safe to ball my eyes out without having to explain to someone why I was balling my eyes out. I was a psychology major at the time and I knew that if I told someone they would just look at me like…*can't you fix yourself?* I had been having anxiety attacks on a regular basis, maybe once a week, at least. I didn't want to tell anyone because I didn't want to be treated like a patient. This particular anxiety attack occurred because of money. My parents could barely afford my tuition and though I was working part-time, it was certainly not enough.

Weeks prior to this particular attack, the housing coordinator at school came into my dorm room and told me that if my parents didn't pay tuition by five o'clock the next day, I had to leave. I felt like I was in some mobster movie and owed the mob some money. She was the gangster and I was the fool stupid enough to get involved in a business deal with a gangster. That day I used my anxiety to work out. I went on a run because I was too nervous to sit still. I called my parents afterwards to tell them what happened. Needless to say, my parents came through the next day and I was able to stay.

On this particular Friday night, however, things had taken a turn. I felt overwhelmed. I didn't want to let my parents down because they worked so hard to keep me in school. I didn't want to fail statistics. I was in statistics II (statistics for social sciences) it was more advanced than intro to statistics (which I passed with a B) and much harder for me to understand. I received my test back and I failed but I was doing my homework, that's the only reason I was hanging on by a thread in that class. It all seems so trivial and pointless now but at the time school felt like the weight of the world on my chest, making it hard for me to breathe. I thought I would fail and I couldn't fail. If I failed a core class I wouldn't be able to graduate in two semesters, I would have to graduate in three. This anxiety attack was not solely based on my statistics test, it was because of the financial pressures my family faced and the fact that if I failed statistics I'd have to take the course again, that was a failure none of us could afford. When I thought of these things, the hyperventilating started. I didn't want to fail and I didn't want to force my parents to continue to work like dogs to pay for my failure. I started crying and the crying turned into sobs, and the sobs made it harder to breathe. I decided to take a shower to calm me down and because I knew no one would be able to hear me sobbing through the walls. And to the shower I brought a razor.

I didn't plan on doing anything with the razor. But then I started thinking about how much easier it would be on my parents if I was dead and how tired I was of fighting for everything. I started to cry, *I'm so tired, I can't do this anymore, God help me.* And then I pressed the razor against my wrist and slid it across. I did it again. And again, pressing harder each time. The final time I jolted my hand back because of the pain. I hadn't felt the pain until that moment and I think it was because I thought to myself, *I can't quit.* A simple quick thought and suddenly I could feel the pain. This was the closest I'd ever come to actually committing suicide, a few little nicks on the wrist that healed in a few days and didn't leave a scar so that I could act like it never happened.

I got out of the shower, looked in the mirror and convinced myself that dying is the easy way out and that I'm not a quitter. Truthfully, I was afraid of the pain; the pain of the cuts that I'd felt when the thought of quitting flashed through my mind and the pain that I would cause my parents and my brothers. I told myself I needed to stick it out, no matter how painful or hard life gets. Then I joked in my head, *how gross would it be for my roommate to find me dead and naked on the shower floor?* I chuckled, wiped my tears, and went to bed. I moved on like nothing happened. I didn't seek help, I didn't tell anyone. I thought it would resolve itself, that I'd be happier once I graduated, I just needed to get through college.

I was afraid of telling this story because I do want to be a psychologist one day and though I'm seeking to specialize in neuropsychology, there is the view that if you want to be a psychologist you have to be mentally perfect. And while I no longer have depression and my anxiety attacks are virtually nonexistent now I still have this fear that because of my past my future is ruined. But I still try, I still move forward and work towards my goals. Personally, I appreciate psychologists who have gone through similar stressors and have overcome many challenges because I view them as stronger than the average psychologist. It would have been easy for me and anyone to write a book about perseverance without adding the gory and uncomfortable details about the lows in life and I considered deleting this chapter entirely because of anxious thoughts about what it could mean for my future if people really knew what I've gone through. But easy and comfortable are not what this book is about. During no point in your fight with anxiety will you be comfortable, I can promise you that. I share this brief story as an example of how bad my anxiety had become not because I want sympathy but because you need to know who I was so that you can understand how I am who I am, how far I've come, and what qualifies me to write a book about anxiety and depression; because as you may have noticed there's no fancy title after my name. I'm just a twenty-something who has struggled with anxiety for most of her life and has finally found a way out and I want to share that way with you.

CHAPTER 6: COMFORT

If you're too comfortable, you may not be where God needs you. That was the message at church one Sunday. I already knew that God never promised a comfortable and safe life, but for some reason I was hearing these words as if it was the first time. They gave me hope, they motivated me. They gave me hope because they told me that just because my life is hard, doesn't mean God isn't there. They motivated me because they told me that I was being prepared for something. I started school in the fall with a new attitude. It was my final semester of college and I still faced the financial problems I had previously faced and my GPA was still low but I didn't to worry about it anymore. I just knew the very fact I was in college was a miracle in itself. My dad and I had a talk before school started and he told me that he really didn't know where the money came from but it always seemed that when our backs were against the wall and we were looking down the barrel, that they were able to come up with the money somehow. I mean, he obviously knew where the money came from (loans, work, pawn shops, etc.) but what he meant was, when it seemed like there was no hope, hope was found in the form of cash coming in randomly, just when they needed it, just when it seemed our cup had run dry. So I knew that I'd be fine. And I was right.

That semester I was told by housing that because my dorm was more expensive than my parents could afford, I would need to move. My choices were: live with a freshman or move out. Well, I had some terrible experiences living with lowerclassmen so I chose the latter. I prayed to God, *please help me find a place to live, you've brought me this far so I have faith.* I didn't know where I would live, but I started searching, I sent a text to my friend because she had an apartment with an extra room and by the next week, I had found a new home. It was an apartment in BloNo or Bloomington-Normal, for those of you who are unfamiliar with the central

Illinoisan term. The apartment was thirty minutes away from school and I drove a Ford minivan, a hand-me-down from my parents that we had since I was ten or eleven. Anyway, this meant that a large portion of the money I made at my job would be for gas and the rest for food, my parents agreed to pay my portion of the rent. With my living situation squared away, I was able to finish school and graduate with my Bachelor's.

After reading about my experience in college you can probably see why I was discouraged about my hospital job. It was a job that I landed that didn't even require a degree. As I've said, it was as if everything that I had gone through was for nothing. As if everything my parents did was for nothing. It was like I failed. My silver lining was graduate school.

I was doing well in my graduate program, I was getting all A's and learning a lot. Because I had been through so much during undergraduate school I fought hard during graduate school and did not coward away. I was very involved and a go-getter. I took a work study so that I could apply what I learned and increase my research skills on top of keeping my internship and maintaining my GPA. I loved my program because it gave me the opportunity to learn by doing. It wasn't until graduate school that I understood the difference between an "S" and an "A" in the B.S. and "B.A." A B.S. is a methodology, scholar based degree while a B.A. is a practitioner based degree, and it's the same with Master's degrees. I was in an M.A. program and I was very good. I discovered that I learn by doing. I had to take a statistics course for the Master's program, it was just as tough as my previous statistics course however, this one was different. I actually got to perform the statistics I was learning about in SPSS. We were given a case study at the beginning of the course about a fictitious company who needed a statistician to run statistics based off the data they collected. Throughout the course we were taught about different statistics and we were able to apply the lessons directly. We were given assignments that required us to create PowerPoints, handouts, videos, etc. as an aim to teach the organization how statistics are useful to them. At the end of the course we had to put together a proposal that communicated to the organization what statistics were run and what the implications of the various results were. The professor gave me feedback about what I could do better and for each assignment I took her criticism and changed my delivery based on what she told me. At the end of the class the professor told me that she was impressed with my growth and appreciated me taking her criticism and changing my methods and structures. I finished the class with an A.

CHAPTER 7: CHANGE OF VIEW

The way I used to think about life was completely different than I the way I think about it now. I used to think life was happening to me. What I mean by that is I used to feel trapped in life, as if I was the victim. Bad things would happen and I didn't understand why I seemed to be having a rough go at life while the people around me seemed to have fewer cares and concerns. Through time and practice I've learned that life is not happening to me; it is not a series of events that inflict upon me. In fact, most of the events that occur in our lives occur because of decisions we or other people have made. I came to realize that once we better understand what is happening, we can come up with a solution to the problem more easily.

Depression and anxiety are constant battles. For many people it is an everyday battle, one that some quit fighting. I believe that for some people there is a way to combat depression and anxiety without medication. Many medications increase suicidal thoughts and have many other risks. As the number of depressed individuals increases one has to wonder if we will all become drugged up drones one day. For some of us, there is another option. We can change our thinking patterns and become less impulsive. Impulsivity is an increasing phenomenon in our society because we are used to quick thinking, immediate service, and just doing it. I learned how our brains learn, remember, and react and this helped me to control my own anxiety. It isn't too difficult to understand and there are resources that I will mention later that can help you as well.

How to Change Your Point of View

It is easy for one to say to someone, "stop being a victim," it is harder to tell someone how to stop being the victim. In this section I give a general outline on how to stop being a victim:

1. Realize that what is happening is due to a series of decisions
   a. These decisions may be yours or someone else's
   b. Think about how these decisions were made
      i. Were they impulsive

        ii. Were they well thought-out
   c. What role did you play in these decisions and how can this impact your future decisions?
2. Think about the big picture
   a. What is the main goal?
   b. How can you obtain this goal?
3. What are the obstacles
   a. How can you overcome these obstacles?
        i. Create sub-steps for how you will overcome each obstacle (these can also be called mini-goals)
4. When obstacles arise, adapt and go back to step one

It is a very simple outline but we have a hard time living it out. It is hard for us to think of the role we may have played in our situations and harder for us to come up with solutions rather than to sulk in our disappointments. But with practice, the above outline will become automatic because your brain will learn that when an obstacle appears, this is the response. Below is a real-life example that I created for myself when I wanted to go to graduate school but was unsure how I would pay for student loans while in school.

1. I had undergraduate student loan debt from going to college, that was my decision.
   a. Taking out student loans was my parents' idea because they could not afford tuition
   b. I made the decision to trust my parents impulsively, they made the decision to take out loans non-impulsively
   c. I let my parents make my financial decisions when I was 18. Now that I am out of college, I need to learn take responsibility for my debt
2. I want to earn a doctorate in psychology
   a. A doctorate in psychology
   b. Go to graduate school
3. Obstacles
   a. Low undergraduate GPA
        i. Get a Master's degree first
        ii. Find an internship to stick out from other applicants
        iii. Research current topics in psychology to find out what the most needed professionals in psychology are & take MOOC (free online) courses that relate to the field
        iv. Update resume
   b. No money

           i. Find a program that will allow me to work and go to school

          ii. Start making payments on loans & interest while they are in deferral status

        iii. Pay for Master's program with student loans

              1. Take work study

         iv. Find Assistantships for doctoral program

4. Recently stopped working full-time

    a. I had to quit my job because it was taking too much of my time and energy, needed to focus on future-oriented activities

         i. This was my decision

              1. This decision was not impulsive; I had been thinking about it for several months

              2. This decision gave me freedom and made me feel more in control of my life

    b. I want to be a psychologist but I also want to make money while in school

         i. Keep my work study

        ii. Become a sole proprietor writer

    c. Obstacles

         i. I do not know much about being a freelance writer

              1. I can research what this means

              2. Research types of writers

              3. Research novellas, novels, short stories, self-help, etc.

              4. Research word counts

              5. Research prices for books

              6. Research prices for podcasts

              7. Create online profile

        ii. How do I start

              1. Start writing what I'm passionate about and see where it goes

As one can see, the outline can become extensive but it is beneficial to visualize where you want to be, assess where you are now, and create a plan when obstacles arise, however that may look for you. For instance, in real life my outline did not look nearly as neat as the above outline, it was cultivation of notes and scribbles on a loose leaf paper. Sometimes, it is even a bunch of doodles and words. Whatever this process looks like for you is fine, as long as you are thinking about your goals, obstacles, and steps.

CHAPTER 8: STOPPING ANXIOUS THOUGHTS

Stopping anxious thoughts will take time and the craft comes with practice. For me it was pivotal that I recognized when my anxiety attacks occurred. When I thought back to previous anxiety attacks I realized that they occurred when I was pressed with unexpected financial debt and when I was presented with uncomfortable social experiences. Examples of when I would get anxiety attacks are: the beginning of every school year because my parents never knew if they would be able to come up with the money for me to go back to school, the end of the semester when I was faced with more financial burdens, and believe it or not, dinner time for my first few semesters at college because that was the time when the whole campus came to the commons to eat food. In fact, I eventually took a job at the commons just to avoid the fear of eating alone in a room full of people. In sum, I noticed that my main triggers were financial burdens and social situations.

Many of us have learned that in order to overcome fears we must face them. I took this line of thinking with me as I signed into my student loan website and came face to face with the debt owed, I figured out how much my salary would be after school was over and how much I would have to pay per month. After realizing that my debt is manageable, I had an easier time tackling other financial obligations such as medical bills, car insurance, etc.

Notice that I did not ask myself, "why is this happening?" and "who's fault is this?" Such questions are what I asked when I was in college and they always led to feelings of hopelessness and depression and further triggered anxiety attacks, thus instilling my behavioral mentality that when financial burdens are present I should shut down. My mind had become so used to the above process of finding blame and playing victim that it was very hard for me to break this pattern. I forced myself to focus on the facts: the fact is I have student debt and I will need to pay this. Stating this fact clearly made it easier for me to find a solution. Think about it, which statement triggers a solution-focused mind: "I shouldn't have gone to college" or "I have student debt and I will need to pay this"? The first statement places blame, I'm blaming myself for this debt because had I not gone to college I wouldn't have debt, this way of thinking is counterproductive. Focusing on would've, could've, should've, doesn't get us very far. The second statement clearly displays what is going on in the present, this makes it easier for me to focus on finding a solution to my problem and keeps me positive because I am not blaming myself or others for the situation I am in, I am instead dealing with what is in front of me.

The second trigger was social situations. Before I begin let me be clear, I do still have social anxiety but it has minimized overtime and is virtually nonexistent. I can now sit in a crowded room and eat alone with no discomfort and I can engage in social interactions with minimal discomfort. As I stated previously, my social anxiety was so horrendous that I would skip dinner. For my first semester at my alma mater I would skip dinner every night that I didn't have a friend to eat with, it wasn't until later in the semester that I found out that there was a second place to eat later at night that wasn't very crowded. But it wasn't just the commons, I had a very hard time talking to the opposite sex, I was afraid of popular people, I didn't speak in class unless I was sure my answer was correct, and my whole first year of high school I had tremors in classes where public speaking was heavy, even if it was a lecture day I'd still sit at my desk shaking like a leaf for the whole 50 minutes. While I think there is value in assessing why people have social anxiety, ultimately finding the origin is only a small part of the battle. The hardest part is confronting the problems in front of you *now*. Therefore, I won't dive into why I think I have social anxiety because my main goal was to just deal with the problem at hand. I wanted to date, I wanted to engage in discussion in class, I wanted to eat when I was hungry! I wanted very normal things but could not seem to bring myself to do those things.

My solution was simple, not easy. Confront the fears while focusing on the facts: date someone, eat alone in public, say something in class regardless of whether it's well thought out or not. The fact about social anxiety is that it is literally a fear of being social, usually because of fear of ridicule. The fact that I reminded myself of while I was attacking my social anxiety-related fears was: "the world is not seeking to hurt me. No one cares if I eat alone. No one will attack me for being myself." While in some cases people do get attacked, logically I doubted that people would attack me for eating alone. I drove fear out by doing what I was afraid of and by reminding myself to be logical and state the facts. Another fact was: "not everyone will like me or agree with me, but I do not need to apologize for being me. I accept myself." This fact was important, because you may have noticed that many socially anxious people apologize a lot; this isn't because they are genuinely sorry for whatever it is they seem to be apologizing for, it is because they are afraid that if they do not apologize they will be rejected, socially attacked, ostracized, or hurt someone's feelings thus ostracizing themselves. You may do this or you may know someone who does; this person may say, "sorry but I just don't…" or laugh and then apologize for laughing. Silly as it may seem, these apologies are techniques socially anxious people use to win favor or dilute a situation they see as threatening because of something they did, said, or will say. Replacing anxiety provoking thoughts with factual thoughts is important, it changes a thought like: "I'm not good enough" to "I need to improve my social skills." The former is a general comment many anxious people say to themselves and it is very broad and indirective, it is stating as fact something that is opinion. The latter is informative and directive and it is stating what I need to work on. It may be true that I'm not good enough at social skills, but the second statement inspires hope that I can become better with work.

Continuing on, I didn't attack all of these fears at once but whenever I saw an opportunity I took it. My mantra was, "if it makes me feel like running in the other direction, I should do it." I practiced being alone in public, I tried to start conversations with freshmen, when I felt anxious in class I spoke my mind, and eventually I dated. After college I knew that I still had a long way to go: adults still made me uncomfortable, leading groups was scary, and I hated being recorded and photographed. That was just two years ago and now my life is very different: I just took a leadership position at church where I lead a small group of about 12 freshmen girls, I recently was "hot-seated" by their parents, they grilled me with questions about myself, the group, how their daughters fit in, how I'm leading them, etc. and I now keep in contact with their parents on a weekly basis. In my work study as a student engagement coordinator my job is literally to engage adults by leading meetings and communicating ideas with them. In addition, I'm currently a contributing editor of curriculum for Best Minds Associates where one of my job roles is to record podcasts of myself speaking.

My advice to anyone with anxiety attacks is to:

- Find the triggers
- Focus on the facts
- Run towards the triggers
- Keep your eyes open for opportunities that scare you and then take those opportunities
- Replace anxious thoughts with facts and hope-provoking language

It is going to be incredibly uncomfortable and you will fail multiple times and you will be awkward. However, once you meet your first achievement you will be addicted to overcoming your fears. Once you come to the conviction that you will overcome your fears, you will be surprised at how many opportunities pop up that allow you to tackle them first hand. For example, a year ago I didn't think I'd be recording podcasts or leading groups or even writing a book but the opportunities presented themselves and I took them.

CHAPTER 9: STOPPING DEPRESSIVE THOUGHTS

Depression is unlike many other illnesses in that symptoms are not physically visible and for many battling depression means changing the way they think. This is not to say that medication is not necessary however I believe that for many people there is another option. Depression looks differently on different people; many people have depressive episodes but are not chronically depressed. For me, I have chronic anxiety that when extreme can lead to depression. Take chapter 5 for example, I had an anxiety attack that enforced depressive thoughts. This happens for me whenever I let anxiety run amok. I become helpless, say 'I can't do this,' I tell myself I'm tired of surviving and that I want to live, I try to find blame, I lose faith, and I regret being born. What happens is that anxiety takes over, reason is no longer present in my mind and all I can think about is how hard my life is and every previous obstacle I've had to face and I start asking myself why I can't seem to catch a break, and why does it seem that I have to fight for everything? This line of thinking goes on for several minutes and then I start trying to find a way out of life, yes I start thinking of suicide. Usually this is the point where I turn my thinking around. But one day in my dorm I started to think, *what if I can't turn it around in time to save myself?* This thought scared me as I imagined laying lifeless on my bed in 20 years as my kids or husband try to wake me up and how they would feel when they realized I wasn't asleep. *I had to do something.*

My life is different now in that most of the time I avoid anxiety attacks and thus don't have depressive episodes. However, it is something that I work at constantly. And to be honest, the way I overcome anxiety is through a combination of my faith and science. Many people believe you must choose one or the other but God created the natural world so why would science and faith not go hand in hand? My understanding of the brain and who God is has helped me battle anxiety and depressive episodes.

The premise of the Bible is that God continuously tries to connect with us and we continuously ignore, push Him away, or get lost because it is natural. Many people think that in order to be a Christian you must be perfect but it's quite the contrary. In fact, Christians are people who realize that they are imperfect but that there is a God who accepts them anyway. Now you may be asking, "but what about all of those sacrifices and obeying the 10 commandments or the other rules?" The truth is Christians struggle with these rules just like anyone else. Many sin on a regular basis. The only difference is, we accept a love and forgiveness that we do not deserve. For me, this makes me *want* to obey Him and the closer I get to Him the easier it is for me to do so. However, this would not have been possible without God sending His Son to die for our sins. This sacrifice exemplified the love of the Father and relinquished our debts. Essentially, the message of the Gospel is this: "for God so loved the world that He gave His only begotten Son so that whoever believes in Him shall not perish but have everlasting life," (John 3:16). And He gave His Son because "the wages of sin is death but the gift of God is eternal life," (Romans 6:23).

So how does this help me? Well these particular verses did not help me with anxiety, they helped me become a Christian and if I were not a Christian I would not read the Bible, if I did not read the Bible I wouldn't get the encouragement I need to keep living in this wrecked world everyday. Essentially, becoming a Christian not only saved my eternity but my physical life as well because I am certain that I would be dead right now if I were not a Christian.

So which verses helped me with depressive thoughts? There are several verses that have helped me and below I've listed a few along with explanations of how they helped me.

- **Luke 8:40-47:** "Now when Jesus returned, a crowd welcomed him, for they were all expecting him. **41** Then a man named Jairus, a synagogue leader, came and fell at Jesus' feet, pleading with him to come to his house **42** because his only daughter, a girl of about twelve, was dying.

As Jesus was on his way, the crowds almost crushed him. **43** And a woman was there who had been subject to bleeding for twelve years, but no one could heal her. **44** She came up behind him and touched the edge of his cloak, and immediately her bleeding stopped.

45 "Who touched me?" Jesus asked.

When they all denied it, Peter said, "Master, the people are crowding and pressing against you."

46 But Jesus said, "Someone touched me; I know that power has gone out from me."

47 Then the woman, seeing that she could not go unnoticed, came trembling and fell at his feet. In the presence of all the people, she told why she had touched him and how she had been instantly healed. **48** Then he said to her, "Daughter, your faith has healed you. Go in peace."

- **James 1:5-8:** "If any of you lacks wisdom, you should ask God, who gives generously to all without finding fault, and it will be given to you. **6** But when you ask, you must believe and not doubt, because the one who doubts is like a wave of the sea, blown and tossed by the wind. **7** That person should not expect to receive anything from the Lord. **8** Such a person is double-minded and unstable in all they do."
- **Proverbs 3:5-6** "Trust in the Lord with all your heart and lean not on your own understanding; **6** in all your ways submit to Him, and He will make your paths straight"

The above passages remind me to keep my faith God. They also point out that without it, I shouldn't expect anything different, I should expect the same results. And quite honestly, when my back is against a wall and I don't know what to do and I ask God for help and have faith in Him, He has not failed me and He never will. God allows trouble to come to us so that we can seek Him and so that when He pulls us through we can tell people about it so that more may come to Him. He also allows trouble to come to us so that our faith in Him is instilled.

- **Luke 9: 57-62 57** "As they were walking along the road, a man said to him, "I will follow you wherever you go."

58 Jesus replied, "Foxes have dens and birds have nests, but the Son of Man has no place to lay his head."

59 He said to another man, "Follow me."

But he replied, "Lord, first let me go and bury my father."

60 Jesus said to him, "Let the dead bury their own dead, but you go and proclaim the kingdom of God."

61 Still another said, "I will follow you, Lord; but first let me go back and say goodbye to my family."

62 Jesus replied, "No one who puts a hand to the plow and looks back is fit for service in the kingdom of God."

The above passage reminds me that following Jesus is not easy, nowhere in the Bible does He promise it will be easy. Following Him will be difficult and when He leads us somewhere we should not hesitate or think twice, but we should go. If we do not do this, we are not fit to serve the Kingdom of God-and that's every Christian's job. So when I feel hesitant to follow Him I think of where my heart is. What is getting in my way? Why would I not go follow and trust someone who has saved me twice? Usually it's fear so I work to tackle those fears.

- **Luke 10:2-3** "He told them, "The harvest is plentiful, but the workers are few. Ask the Lord of the harvest, therefore, to send out workers into his harvest field. **3** Go! I am sending you out like lambs among wolves."

The above passage exemplifies EXACTLY what it is to be a Christian in the world. We *are* lambs among wolves. This verse reminds me that I am going through this season, this anxiety, this depression, this situation, this death, for a reason. I am a lamb among wolves and I will hurt but I am here for a purpose. When I was having an anxiety attack followed by a depressive episode one day I grabbed my Bible and read my devotional and wouldn't you know it, Luke 9 & 10 were the passages I was supposed to read that day. I read these passages and immediately prayed, "I'm sorry for my lack of faith. This world wrecks me but you've chosen *this* soul for a reason. You've brought me here and I will not leave before my purpose is fulfilled." I started to view suicide as quitting on God and saying to Him, "you've chosen the wrong person, I can't do this." If this is hard for you to grasp because you're not a believer, imagine this: the President and the country need your help for something and you're the only one in the entire country with the particular set of skills and experiences that can help. Imagine the President and the country are giving and faithful to you, never letting you down, always there when you need them. Imagine being sent to the White House only to look this faithful, giving, loving President in the eyes and say, "I can't do this, you've chosen the wrong person," and walking away. It's kind of hard to look someone who has given you everything in the eyes and say 'no' especially when there is so much at stake.

There are many other verses and I could write a book about all of the verses that have helped me. Instead, I will list a few stories and books and encourage you to read them on your own and see what they mean for you.

- Genesis chapter 27 through chapter 33. Pay close attention to the story of Jacob's betrayal and forgiveness as well as the story of Leah
- Esther
- Proverbs
- Job
- And of course, the Gospels: Matthew, Mark, Luke, and John. These are the stories of Jesus from four different perspectives and to different audiences.

Continuing, science has shown that positive people live longer, have fewer health problems, have better sex lives, etc. From a psychology standpoint we know that positive people who persevere tend to have better quality of lives. From books we learn that being positive is key. However, few people can tell us *how* to be positive in a way that is clear to us. "Just stop thinking negatively," is not good advice. People who are depressed do not wake up every day *wanting* to be depressed, they just can't seem to be anything but depressed. Churches will tell you to read your Bible, psychologists will tell you to work on key characteristics, I'm telling you to do both. The constant work that psychologists tell us we need to do in order to grow coupled with the positive reinforcement and encouragement of the Bible is the anecdote that can change everything. I used to wake up every day disappointed that I survived another night, it used to be that bad for me. Here are the psychological practices that helped change my life:

- **Facts:** again, stating the facts helps me keep things in perspective. Example: I need this amount of money but don't have it. What are the options? What is worse case? What is best case? This is the most important step because you are reminding yourself of what is real and what has been fabricated in your mind. In addition, it forces you to say to yourself, "this is what is happening right now. I have to deal with it, it's not going to go away. This is my life and I need to face it."
- **Solution-finding:** Sometimes there is no solution however, just looking for a solution can help.
- **Planning**: How will I realistically reach the solution I came up with? If there is no solution, now what? How am I going to deal with this?

For those with chronic depression I suggest seeing a psychologist regularly as well as performing the above steps when faced with a difficult scenario. In addition, I suggest taking these steps daily:

- **Talking to yourself:** We all do it and it's actually healthy. Whether this looks like writing yourself a note the night before so that you can read it in the morning or whether it's looking at yourself in the mirror and saying something, it is beneficial to say at least this: "I accept myself no matter what." This constant reminder will help you to eventually accept who you are and will make you more comfortable being yourself because you know your love for yourself is not conditional. The same can be said for God's love for us so you can also start with: "I am fearfully and wonderfully made" (Psalms 139:14).
- **Exercise, Sleep, Food:** I actually suggest this to anyone and everyone regardless of if you're depressed or not. 20 minutes of cardio a day. 20 minutes of cardio increases blood flow in the brain, mood, and obviously makes you physically healthier in the long run as well. I'm sure we've heard that sleep and diet also play a role in our mental health. There is scientific evidence that supports

this but it is common sense, really; how can your brain function well if you're not taking care of it?

- **Be Social:** As an introvert I hate when people tell me this. However, I mean it differently than most people. I don't mean be outgoing and go party. I mean find something you enjoy and find other people who enjoy that thing and go do it. Join a book club, go to church, join a choir, dance, play intermural sports, etc. And I know this can be especially hard to do when we're feeling depressed. When you're having a depressive episode take your reluctance to be around people as a sign that you *should* be around people. Do it for at least an hour and see how you feel afterwards.

- **Be honest:** Telling a few trusted people, about your struggles will help you. We weren't meant to be alone and we do need people. But you also need to be honest with yourself. If you are depressed, do not try to pretend that everything is okay. If you do this, you are denying the truth and you will not reach resolution this way; in the long run it will catch up to you.

- **Purpose:** Remind yourself that you have a purpose. If you don't know what it is, start with what you love to do and see where it takes you.

- **Destroy:** Stop damaging thoughts before they destroy your confidence. We usually know what our insecurities are and focusing only on our faults does not help us. I am all for self-improvement, but you need to know the difference between self-improvement and self-destruction. A simple comment like, "ugh I am gross I need to lose weight" can destroy this person overtime. While a comment like, "I need to lose weight" can motivate this person to set a goal, "okay I'm going to try to lose ten pounds in five months." The first comment sets a deconstructive criticism that may lead to more negative thoughts like, "no one will ever find me attractive." The second states a fact, "I need to lose weight." Now this person can think, "okay, I've stated the fact, now I can create a plan to achieve this," and just like that, their fact becomes a goal instead of a criticism.

Keep in mind that this chapter is just the beginning for you, you still have a long way to go and should always continue to research, practice, and fight.

CHAPTER 10: LEARNING GRIT

In my life I have learned and grown and stretched in ways I didn't think I could. What has gotten me to where I am today is not a perfect resume, perfect GPA, perfect family, or perfect anything. I am not exceptional in most things, I am not one of kind, I am determined. What has brought me to this point in my life is my reluctance to quit. When everything else in my life points to me not achieving something or not doing something; when everything says I should fail, when it seems like there is no way I can succeed, I do anyway. I achieve, I perform, I execute. How? Why? Because I have grit. I have learned that there are two kinds of grit: there are the people who get out of their own way and succeed and there are the people who get in their own way and succeed anyway. I was the second kind of person and it took a lot of work for me to become the first kind of person. Maybe you aren't either kind of person, maybe you don't have grit at all, in that case you should especially finish reading this chapter.

Let me begin with the person who gets in their own way and succeeds anyway. These individuals are determined but doubtful. These people have a vision for who they want to be, what they want to achieve and how they want to get there. But they have doubts in their heads. These doubts tell them they're not smart enough, not outgoing enough, too outgoing, not compassionate enough, not poised enough, etc. These people act out the plans to achieve their goals to prove to themselves they can do it. They're their own worse critic. This was me. Part of it had to do with my anxiety. I would remind myself why I couldn't be who I wanted, "that wouldn't work because I'm too shy." And part of it had to do with lack of confidence in my capabilities, "I'm not smart enough for that." And if I did have the nerve to succeed do you think my inner voice was silenced by success? Of course not, it would say, "well that only worked because I tricked them into thinking I'm someone I'm not." That's right, these types of people battle themselves constantly because their actions conflict with their thoughts. Not only do these people have to overcome obstacles that come their way in life but they also have to overcome their own self-doubt and ridicule. There are various reasons why people do this to themselves: they may not believe they deserve what they want, they may not want to get their hopes up about good things to come, they may even feel guilty about something. If this is you, my homework for you is to ask yourself "why?" Why ridicule and doubt yourself and your steps? Why steal away the joy of your successes? My second set of homework is for you to ask yourself, "is it helpful?" Does it slow you down, does it motivate you? This is a self-destructive pattern and completely unnecessary. I'm not saying that you should become prideful but I am saying that you need to become aware of your thoughts and how those thought make you feel and how those feelings influence your actions.

Continuing, the first person does not get in their own way but overcomes outside obstacles with a healthy mentality. This is the person I am now. These people do not shy away from obstacles, they do not fear hardships, they do not crumble at a dissolved plan, they adapt and try again. The reason that this is such a hot topic today is because we hear stories of people who have gone through the worst things and succeed anyway and we're fascinated. We're fascinated because grit is unnatural. Our very nature is to run or fight when we are hurt or threatened. This is easy to visualize when we're picturing a boxing match but hard to execute when we're living our lives. When we make plans for our careers and they fall through, when we put time and energy into a relationship and are betrayed, when we apply ourselves in school and don't get the results, it is easiest to run. It's easier to quit a business venture than to try again, it's easier to move out than to sleep in the same bed, it's easier to quit school than to graduate. Why is this? It is because we avoid pain. If this is you, I urge you to read the story of Jacob in the Bible. It's a natural response to run; when we touch something too hot we quickly move our hands away because it's painful. Our pain receptors tell us when we are doing something damaging to our bodies. But our minds work a little differently, our brains respond to pain **but** that pain is *interpreted* in our minds-this is where we decide what to do about that pain. Physical pain triggers instant reaction, you get away from the stimulus because it's threatening your life or comfort. Psychological pain triggers the same chemical response as when we feel physical pain however, with psychological pain we have the ability to construct a non-impulsive response to the pain. This takes time to develop because the mind is used to responding a certain way because that's how it has responded for so many years but the more you practice grit, the easier grit comes to you-it becomes almost impulsive with practice. Here is how you learn grit:

- Stop destructive thinking, do this by nipping it in the bud immediately. Imagine yourself achieving your goal. Think about the details of this goal. Tell yourself you will do it, not that you can do it but that you *will* do it. Shut the doubtful thoughts out by believing that you are capable. And if you don't believe you are capable then list the characteristics that would make you capable and then achieve them.

- <u>Discouragement</u>: It is okay to become discouraged but don't stay there for more than a few minutes. That's all you're allowed, a few seconds to be upset, a few more to get angry, a few more to sulk. Then the time is up. Being discouraged is a natural response, being sad and angry are normal but you can't live in those emotions. If you live in those emotions, (allow those emotions to become your attitude) you will get nothing done and you'll do psychological damage to yourself in the long-run. Be sad, get angry, cry, yell, do what's naturally but then get back to the drawing board.

- <u>Remind yourself</u> of your goal daily. It is important that you remind yourself what you're working towards, especially during hard times.

- <u>Read</u> uplifting, motivational literature. I read my Bible because there are various stories of people who overcame obstacles and various verses from God himself who encourages us to live.

- <u>Connect</u> with determined individuals. In your friendships it is important that you are around people who are ambitious and determined. It is hard to stay focused on a goal when the people around you have given up trying. I'm not saying to end those friendships but to find new friends who have grit. You will get a contact high just by being around them and then you may end up motivating friends who have given up. Another good way to do this is through social media. If you don't feel comfortable following people on Twitter, Instagram, or Snapchat then you can just search for them and meander through their social media pages every once in a while. I will admit, I do this sometimes because there are some celebrities whose social media accounts spread motivation and inspiration. If you don't know where to start try: pastors, psychologists, athletes, writers, actors, etc.

- <u>Practice</u>: You **MUST** practice grit every day, it is not optional. If you want to achieve, if you want thick skin, you have to do this. Take chances and if you fail, get over it and try another tactic. Invite failure into your life and you'll stop being afraid of it. Take a chance on yourself and fail and hurt so that you can practice grit. I'm not saying that failure will eventually stop hurting, I'm saying that what once was an unbearable, embarrassing, burning and stabbing at the heart will become a sting overtime. You will one day fail and you will say, "that didn't work...okay what's next?" You will learn to adapt and grit will be second nature. And yes, maybe five years from now you will experience a failure, a loss that feels a lot like that first failure or loss-a burning, stabbing, unbearable pain. But, you will be better equipped to handle it.

- <u>Celebrate:</u> We often get so caught up in achieving and overcoming that we forget to celebrate success because we get caught up in the next goal. I hardly celebrated graduating college because the next goal was finding a job. It wasn't until recently, when I took my cousin to get her driver's license that I realized how little I have celebrated achievements. Here I am at the DMV and she's smiling ear to ear, praising God, texting everyone, and making plans to celebrate passing a driver's test and I've barely celebrated graduating college, getting into graduate school, or finishing my first year in graduate school with a 3.9. I've thanked God but I haven't praised Him by enjoying the fruits of my labor and I haven't praised Him by celebrating with friends. I enjoy working hard and moving onto the next goal and I like not resting on my laurels. But friends, while it's okay to be ambitious it's also healthy to rest your mind and body. Even the Lord took a break.

CHAPTER 11: GRIT & DEPRESSION

I have dreams sometimes about people I don't know, people who have given up. They are going through something hard and they're struggling to come out of it. My most recent dream was about a girl I've never seen before, she was overweight and very pretty and at first she was happy, her day was going well. But then something happened, some rejection that made her sink into old insecurities. She got out of bed and started to hyperventilate, she started crying. She went into her bathtub with a blade and cried, "okay, okay, good girl, good girl," as she cut her arms, and then I woke up. Now this is a total work of fiction made up by my sleeping mind. I know that, but still I can't help but think, *someone somewhere is doing this, someone is hurting themselves because they don't know how to cope. Someone is suffering.*

Having grit plays a large role in overcoming depression. Depression is debilitating, it requires and demands your strength, your time, your energy. Depression requires your attention too, it requires you to lose interest in things that you enjoy, it demands all of you. Living with depression is exhausting and at times people want to give up fighting it, sometimes people do give up. People give up not only fighting it but they also give up things they enjoy and distance themselves from the people they love. Fighting depression requires grit. You need to decide you want to survive and overcome it, that's the very first step. If you don't have the conviction to overcome depression, then you can search high and low for a solution but you will remain stuck where you are right now. Make a decision today, do you want to overcome depression or allow it to overcome you? If you choose the former I can help you, if you choose the latter I cannot.

Assuming you've chosen the former, let's continue. Let me begin by stating that depression is in fact a mental disorder (in case you didn't know) and like most mental disorders it is not something that just goes away. There are no magic pills to make you happy all the time, there is no one book that can cure it. If you have depression you will continuously be "battling depression" just as a recovering addict will continuously be recovering. It is a disorder, it is either wired or learned and while in many cases we can unlearn depression, it comes with practice and time and consistency. Allowing yourself the time to grow and develop are very important factors in overcoming depression. With the increase in speed of services and technology, we have come to expect things to occur on demand, we want results at the click of a button. But depression doesn't work this way, you need to take baby steps everyday and realize that any movement towards your goal is a milestone. Maybe for you just getting out of bed and looking in the mirror without a negative thought is a milestone. Maybe being able to take the time to appreciate yourself is a milestone. Maybe just being honest with yourself, that you're not okay, is a milestone. Every night you need to think about what you did yesterday and ask yourself if you were any better today.

Some days will be bad days, but just acknowledging that it's a bad day may be all you need to do that day. One of the things that seem to confuse many people is the difference between a positive mindset and positivity. When we hear the work 'positivity' we often all think of the same things, 'it's the person who smiles all the time, the person who never has anything bad to say, the person who is always excited.' As an idealistic cynic, I used to think these people were fake, walking around in masks they've painted on themselves because no one is that happy about everything all the time so I didn't trust them. However, these people do exist and some of them are not pretending, it's called an expressive personality-they act excited because they are excited. However, only a portion of the population has this personality factor, therefore some people are faking it. They're faking it because some misguided, misinformed person they knew told them to be more positive but didn't really tell them how. This person just said, "you need to be more positive, Mary" and walked away. So now Mary walks around with a fake smile and fake politeness doing things she doesn't really care about and having conversations that don't really interest her because someone told her, "be more positive." When I hear people say this I cringe. It's not that simple, especially if you have depression.

What Mary's friend really meant to tell her is that she needs to have a positive mindset. People with positive mindsets are honest with themselves and with those around them. They may be experiencing a depressive episode; it may have been very difficult for them to get out of bed this morning but they did because they have grit. And not only did they get out of bed but they proceeded to go to work and be an active participant in their lives. Some people think that if they just find the will to go to work that they've won, the battle is over. On the contrary, the battle is still in progress. You must not check out. For example, I have been in depressive episodes where I did not want to be at work, I did not want to be around people, and I did not care about the work. I noticed this pattern in myself when work became stressful and eventually learned to divert my attention. One day something just clicked in me, I went to work with a depressive mood and while a coworker interacted with me I realized I didn't care about anything she was saying, the conversation was boring to me so I chose one thing in the conversation that she said and I went with it, I asked a question that might raise my interest if she answered it. She was talking about her dog and I simply asked, "your dog is your baby, isn't it?" My theory held true, while I was bored about the details of her dog I was interested in the relationship she had with it. Notice I didn't rudely change the subject, I didn't ignore her, I didn't even show disinterest. In fact, I'm pretty sure she thought I was interested, and I was once she answered my question. This may seem like a tangential piece of information but it has meaning, relationships are important, had I just allowed her to talk on and on while I ignored the information she shared, we would eventually have grown apart; I would have essentially been gradually giving up on that relationship because of depressive symptoms. When you are depressed giving up can occur so subtly that you don't even realize. Giving up can come in the form of disinterest, an apathetic feeling, a rejected call, an ignored message, it can even come in the form of working instead spending time with people who care about you.

People with depression and grit have a positive mindset. They take notice of the little things; they are mindful about their feelings, they understand their emotions, they know that if they wake up one day and it is a 'bad day' that they have a little more work to do. They know that on 'bad days' they must be more vigilant of their actions and responses and they know that they must be more attentive than they feel like being. I am not the poster child of positivity and I know that positivity is not the answer, telling a depressed person to be positive is like telling a sprinter to run faster. If when you started this book you thought that I was going to fix your depressive and anxiety problems in a few thousand words, then I'm sorry to disappoint you but this battle is going to take work on your end every single day. My role is to supply you with the information you need to start or continue this battle, my role is to support you. Don't give up; engage in conversations, engage in your work, answer messages that you don't feel like answering, go out with friends when you want to push them away. You have to fight your depressive instincts; you have to have grit to even begin this journey. And if you've bought this book because you want to overcome depression, let me congratulate you because you have it, it was your *grit* that told you to buy this book in the first place. It was your *grit* that told you to even look for help.

CHAPTER 12: GRIT & ANXIETY

Just as with depression, grit plays a large role in overcoming anxiety as well and in some of the same ways. Take my story as an example, I had anxiety when I ate alone, met new people, walked into a crowd, had to deal with bills or finances, etc. Anxiety made my relationships difficult, school difficult, learning difficult, everything was more difficult when I had anxiety on my back. Being anxious is exhausting but I did not give up trying to find ways to overcome anxiety. Once I did find a way that works I found out that grit doesn't stop at finding a way, it continues through your life until anxiety is a nonissue. Once I found out how to diminish and relinquish anxiety, I noticed how consistent and persistent I had to be day-to-day. Most of my social anxiety I had been working on since high school; I was terrified of trying out for sports teams and I did anyway, in college I tried out for cheerleading but tried to be secretive about it because if I didn't make the team, I didn't want people finding out I'd even tried. I consistently did things that scared me because the alternative-not doing anything was too depressing to consider. As an adult, my anxiety is geared more towards financial troubles, as I mentioned previously. This is a little trickier to tackle and required more than just doing what scared me; it required me to get to the root of my anxiety. When I say root I do not mean root cause, I mean asking questions like, 'what is anxiety, how does it influence my physical and mental health, how does it work?' I figured if I could answer those questions I could figure out how to extinguish it.

There are various readings that I will list later that can give you in-depth details about anxiety but in sum, anxiety is a nervous disorder that influences not only your mind but your heart and your brain. If you are not familiar with sensation and perception I will explain it briefly here: sensation is what occurs when your body comes into contact with the outside world, such as when you touch something, when the sensors in your eyes see light, when the sound waves travel into your ears and your ears pick up the sound, etc. Perception is when your brain interprets what you see, those lights are a banana, those sounds are music, etc. Anxiety works in a similar way. Our sensation works the same however, once the stimulus is interpreted by the brain the mind pulls from previous experiences and those experiences may trigger anxiety. And guess what? This new experience is then stored into long-term memory because of the strong emotional response and it will be pulled later when a similar stimulus presents itself therefore, the cycle continues. I've learned how to break this cycle.

I will explain how I broke the cycle but first, let me explain why it is so important to try to overcome anxiety, if you struggle with it. You may think, "what's the big deal, I'm not trying to end my life, it's not as serious as depression." On the contrary, it is as serious because prolonged anxiety can lead to depression. Can you imagine being anxious everyday for the rest of your life? Can you imagine having to tailor what you do all the time and to be at the beck and call of your anxiety? This would exhaust you and would become depressing overtime. Not only can anxiety lead to depression but is related to heart disease. How? Because anxiety strains our hearts unnecessarily, when we are anxious our blood pressures and pulse rise and our hearts beat faster. Why? When anxiety is key for survival (such as during a disaster) our hearts pump faster in order to supply more blood to body parts that need it such as our limbs and certain parts of our brains such as the occipital lobe and the motor cortex. This increased blood flow allows us to run, fight, and pay close attention to life-threatening things. So anxiety, at its core is not bad, it is a survival technique but when anxiety works its way into average situations such as giving a speech, meeting new people, being in a crowded place, etc. it becomes counterproductive because your body and brain are in survival mode when they don't need to be. So of course, this puts stress on the heart. As for "why?" there are various reasons that people develop anxiety: it can be because of previous trauma (PTSD), it can be because of personality; for example, people with type A personality (my personality type), are more likely to develop anxiety. It can also be because of drug or alcohol abuse, genetics, stress, or it can develop because of other illnesses. These are all things that I have learned overtime therefore I encourage you to research these facts for an increase in understanding.

Continuing, first, you need to discover what the cause(s) of your anxiety is, not the triggers but the cause(s). I discovered that my anxiety is partially due to my personality- as you may know, type A personalities are forward thinkers, planners, anticipators, and generally detailed. I'll give you an example, when I was in the eighth grade I had my course-load planned for all four years of high school. Now of course, this does not mean that all type-A people have anxiety, just that we are more likely to develop it. I also realized my anxiety stems mostly from mild PTSD. You may think PTSD is something only military professionals develop but this common thought cannot be farther from the truth. In fact, many people suffer from variations of PTSD. Rape victims, physical assault victims, emotional assault victims, and psychological assault victims can also suffer from PTSD. Before you start to think that I've just diagnosed myself, I did go see a psychologist in college in order to talk through my anxiety and find the root cause, she is the one who told me that my anxiety is a result of very mild PTSD. Let's revisit my anxiety triggers for a moment: social situations and financial stress. Let's revisit my past: being bullied every day from a very young age up until I moved to the suburbs and my father's financial struggle after he was laid off when I was in high school. Let me back up a bit and explain PTSD a bit more. It is a disorder that occurs when an individual has experienced a traumatic event. While in the past bullying hasn't been seen as traumatic it actually is, it is psychological and emotional abuse and it can lead to traumatic injury. And watching a loved one go through a significantly difficult time can also be a traumatic experience because of the emotional strain. Let me back up even further and discuss pain in more detail. When we think of pain we think of physical pain, probably because it is the easiest to understand because we can see it. But psychological and emotional pain can be just as debilitating as physical pain is in that when we experience psychological or emotional pain our brains release some of the same chemicals as it does when we are in physical pain. Not only does it release these chemicals but it also registers this event into long-term memory because of the strong emotional response to the event. This means that when I was bullied, those events were perceived as very painful and were registered into long-term memory. Therefore, I *learned* to be afraid of social interactions because I was afraid of rejection and embarrassment because my brain wanted to avoid the previous pain I felt years ago. And of course any time I did interact with other and it led to pain, I only reinforced this fear and pain-avoidance. The same with financial trouble, because I saw how much it influenced my parents I was afraid of having the same fate so any large and unexpected bill I received triggered anxiety attacks. Again, at its core, this phenomenon is not bad; just as we learn that fire is hot or to put an oven-mitt on when getting something out of the oven, we learn how to avoid psychological and emotional pain too. It is supposed to help us, but sometimes bleeds into everyday situations. For example, I see this a lot when people are dating. A guy or girl has been hurt by a certain type of person before therefore they seek to date someone who is not like that person. But when their current partner shows similarities to their ex they start to question their partner's character. Or a situation arises that requires one person to be more vulnerable but that person is reluctant to be vulnerable because they've been hurt before and this reluctance triggers an argument. Unbeknownst to both parties the invulnerable person's brain is trying to protect itself from being hurt, because the past has taught it that vulnerability leads to pain. I encourage you to pour into research on pain and the brain because you'll start to see the relevancy in everyday life.

Despite the fact that pain-avoidance is wired into our brains, we can learn how to rewire it. Just as I said I *learned* to be afraid of social situations and financial strain, I can also unlearn those fears, and I have. Okay *now* I will tell you how to unlearn anxiety. To start, you need to identify the root and understand it more, examine it because once you understand the condition that your brain and mind are under it becomes easier to heal. Just as with anything, we cannot fix it until we know what's going on. Next, depending on the root you can develop a plan. Clearly this book will not help someone who has anxiety due to alcohol or drug withdraws but it can help someone with social anxiety or anxiety due to mild trauma. Those who have anxiety due to extreme trauma (such as combat or disasters or criminal assaults) or drugs and alcohol need clinical counseling and this book will not be enough. If you are not in those groups the next steps will help you.

Next Steps: Grit

You've learned about your brain and how your anxiety works now how do you tackle it?

- Don't be ashamed of what you're dealing with, seek out people who will be supportive and not ridicule you.
- When you feel an anxiety attack coming, step away for a few moments and breathe saying to yourself, "it's okay, I can do this."
- Stay factual: I've said this before and I'll say it again, *facts, facts, facts matter*! If you feel an anxiety attack coming, state the facts: I'm at a party I'm nervous because there are a lot of people I don't know. I'm afraid of them because… Stating the facts will lead you to realize how irrational your fear is, it reminds you of what is *really* going on instead of allowing you to focus on negative possibilities fabricated by your mind. I cannot stress enough how important this step is. This can mean the difference between you running away or staying.
- Sleep, Exercise, Food: I've discussed how important these three are consistently and I'm sure you've heard it all before. A brain that is sleep deprived is going to be harder to rewire, exercise boosts mood and decreases anxiety, a healthy diet provides nutrition to the brain so that it has the energy and attentiveness necessary to rewire or relearn. Need I say more?
- Don't run from the anxiety: see through the situation. You may have to step away for a minute, you may cry, you may sweat but do whatever you have to do to stay present.
- Practice & Repeat: Just because you overcame an anxious situation does not mean you've relearned anything but it does mean you'll face less resistance by your brain the next time you encounter a similar situation. You have to keep at it repeatedly. If you have social anxiety the only way to

truly heal from it is to expose yourself to social situations regularly. Start small, small talk, introductions, sometimes even just being present and staying for the duration of the event is enough to decrease resistance by your brain.

- Be present: Focus on what is happening now instead of what could happen and what you're afraid of happening. Be present in conversations by asking questions and sharing experiences that tie into what the conversation is about.

- Fight the Urge to Plan: I'm not saying planning is bad but often people with anxiety plan every detail of an encounter. We think about what we'll say, how we'll say it, what we'll wear when we're saying it, how we'll stand, what facial expressions to make, what questions to ask. Doing some of this is okay, for example going over questions to ask or what you'll say in an interview. However, being this extensive for a casual encounter is unnecessary and can lead to anxiety attacks. Take it one step at a time and when in a conversation with someone do not plan what you will say next while they are talking. I must say I still have to fight this tendency oftentimes but I have seen a lot of progress in this area. Just listen to what they're saying and if you get stuck and don't know what to say you can either: sum up what they said while leading into another topic or pick something of interest that they said and ask about it.

- Choose everyday: Decide everyday and at various points during the day that you will not be at anxiety's beck and call. Be mindful of when a situation presents itself for you to create a new neural pathway so that your brain learns a new way to respond to a trigger. Once you continue to strengthen this pathway through repetition (for example, repeatedly introducing yourself to strangers instead of avoiding new people) your brain will learn that the situation is not threatening. I would say that after the first few times of performing an anxiety-provoking behavior you may start to get more comfortable, you will still feel resistance but it will be substantially less from the first time.

These tips may seem to be very few but most of battling anxiety is repetition and practice. You have to, have to, *have to* practice. If you overcome an anxiety-provoking situation one day that does not mean that tomorrow, you get a pass because your brain will just revoke into old patterns of strong and reinforced neural pathways while the new pathway you created today weakens and that's not what we want.

CHAPTER 13: STIGMAS, GRIT & FORGIVENESS

We also need to have grit when dealing with societal stigmas. When people learn that someone has a mental illness, disorder, or challenge, they rely on preconceived notions to direct how they should behave and what they should say. If you are struggling with depression or anxiety, it is important to have grit when telling family members and friends. Many people are either unsure how to behave or they don't want to deal with it. There are even people who will tell a friend to stop being depressing or they become frustrated when their friend posts things on social media, deeming them attention grabby and needy. You shouldn't have to be concerned with how people will receive your battle, you have enough going on in your mind already and being concerned with these things just increases anxiety by triggering thoughts such as, 'maybe I'm a bad friend, maybe I am being attention grabby, maybe I do need to just keep it to myself.' These are all false thoughts and if someone does make you feel this way find someone else to confide in. Generally, people do not know when they are being hurtful to someone who is struggling with a mental issue so you may also want to point it out by expressing how what they say hurt you, forgive them, and as I said find someone you can rely on. There are people who turn to social media and while I condone publicly being yourself and being honest I also think it is more important to find at least one person to turn to for emotional support.

Emotional support increases our abilities to push through obstacles and people who have emotional support are more likely to beat diseases, achieve a goal, and survive a difficult circumstance. In fact many people find what they are going through to be more bearable when they have a friend or family member that is available to listen and help. If you have no one in your life that understands, educate them by telling them what you're struggling with and the ways it has influenced your life. Tell them your anxiety triggers, tell them what anxiety is, tell them your depressive symptoms, make them understand what you're dealing with. People who truly love you will want to help and they'll want to know what you're going through.

When you come across a stigma educate people about the truth. Many people only believe what they hear without doing any digging themselves because it's impersonal to them. However, if they knew there was someone in their circle of friends that struggles with the very thing they're being ignorant about, they will be more inclined to listen and understand. For example, my goal is to be a psychologist. In the African American community people often attribute psychologists to crazy people; they think you're insane or that you will become insane because you're constantly dealing with insane people. This is what I grew up believing and it wasn't until college that I realized there are many types of psychologists that work in diverse places. I also learned that those "insane" people have disorders with names and that strides are being made in the field of psychology in treating those disorders. And now that family members know that I study psychology they ask questions about where I want to work, what kind of psychologist I want to be, etc. I tell them that I want to be a neuropsychologist with integration in industrial and organizational psychology and they ask me what those are and how I plan to incorporate both in my career. The point is that I did not hate psychologists and neither did my family. I just didn't know much about psychologists or the subject of psychology and neither did my family. But notice how once they found out someone close to them is studying psychology, they were eager to understand the subject and my studies and goals. The same is true for mental illness stigmas, people rely on what they've been told and hold it as truth therefore when you hear a stigma understand that it is born of ignorance on the subject and then, educate the person. The more knowledge you have on a subject, the more responsible you are to educate others on that subject; part of this takes grit because you have to keep pushing forward and not give into lies. It takes grit because it requires you not to become discouraged by what people say but inspired by what they can learn from you. It also takes forgiveness because in order to become inspired by what you can teach others you need to first forgive them for what they've said or done to you.

CHAPTER 14: SURVIVING TODAY

When I was a child everyone had a Walkman, by the time I was about ten or eleven we had portable CD players, when I was 14 we had iPods and cell phones that could carry music. When I was in middle school and high school Myspace an IM were cool, by the time I was a senior in high school everyone had a Facebook and now, as a youth group leader my fourteen year old students are always on Snapchat. With the advancement in technology has come the advancement in depressive and anxiety disorders and symptoms. I'm not stating that one causes the other but that there is a clear link between social media and mental health. I've spoken with many people who believe social media is poison however this is not what I believe. When used correctly social media can be an effective tool. Many activists, artists, and writers use social media to publicize injustices. There are things that I never would have known, people whose stories I never would have heard if it weren't for social media. I encourage people to use social media as a tool of encouragement and discovery. With many people who are struggling, the writing is on the wall…on their Facebook walls and it is a great way to connect and reach out and tell someone that you understand what they're going through. Social media is an amazing tool because it can either build people up or literally tear them apart. Cyberbullying has led to suicide attempts and acts of physical violence. On the flip side social media has also created a way for victims and activists to connect in an effort to support one another and to create organizations for people like themselves. I first heard of To Write Love on Her Arms through Facebook when I was a freshman in college and I used their crisis texting services years later in my junior year of college. I was having another financially-linked anxiety attack and I was thinking about how I could escape the never-ending torture that seemed to be my life. I picked up the phone and started texting one of their counselors. She asked me questions about what was going on and how I had contemplated ending my life. I eventually ended up just going to sleep that night. I just needed someone to talk to, someone who didn't know anything about me or who I was. It helped. So another thing that I suggest for someone whose anxiety is so active that it leads you to contemplate suicide is to text a crisis line while in an attack. When I was in college I had the number in my phone just in case I needed it and I only used it once but it was there. Don't be afraid to reach out for help, don't be ashamed of what you're going through because when you think about it logically there is nothing to be ashamed of.

I also encourage you to find a hobby, a way of expression, not a way of distraction. When I was in college I started a blog not directly related to anxiety but related to relationships and it encouraged me to read from strangers who understood me and had gone through similar struggles, it was also just really fun and relieving to sit and write. If you like to dance, dance, if you enjoy writing, write, a singer should sing. Maybe you're not artistic at all but there is something in this world that makes you feel at peace when you're doing it, maybe it's sports or solving a difficult problem/equation, whatever it is make it a priority to do it at least three to four times a week.

But the biggest thing that has helped me survive is God. I cannot stress enough how much I know that if I did not have a close relationship with the Lord that I would not have made it past college. I physically would not have survived college. What I'm saying is I would be cold, in the ground, lifeless, dead. I would not exist. The message of the Gospel is a beautiful tribute to what life is to be like and how we are to survive it. Jesus was betrayed, wrongfully arrested, tormented, tortured, spat on, beaten, and killed. And still He rose. Job was put through the ringer and survived. Nehemiah was threatened and assaulted while trying to keep his people safe. Esther was made to be queen only to risk her life trying to save her people. Leah was unloved by a husband who was tricked into marrying her but found the love she sought in God. Jacob was a betrayer to the people who trusted him and he found strength to reconcile with God the Lord forgave him as did his brother. These are my favorite Bible stories because these people's lives speak a testament to strength, endurance, grit, and faith in God who has never faltered. I used to think that I was being punished when bad things happened, then I read the Bible and realized I was being prepared for things to come.

HELPFUL RESOURCES

Some helpful resources are:

- The Bible! As I've mentioned before, this is a great resource. The Lord presents Himself to those in need, He is the God of the broken.

- Bestmindsassociates.com I did intern with them and do currently work as a freelance curriculum editor and writer but I am paid a flat rate for the work I do and do not receive any special compensation or branding or anything else for promoting them. I promote them because their methods have helped change my life. The way that the psychologists teach you how your brain works, how it works under stress, and how to extinguish anxiety are phenomenal. I've told you how to start breaking the anxiety cycle but their resources give you an in-depth look at your anxious brain and how to rewire it. I suggest going on their website and meandering through their free resources page first, on the left side there is a list of links that you should start pouring through, and then take it from there.

- To Write Love on Her Arms (TWLOHA) is a great resource if you are struggling with depression or want to get involved in activism.

- Willow Creek Community Church is an excellent resource if you live in the Chicagoland area. There are classes, counselors, pastors, small groups, career assistance, etc. If you do not live in the area you can visit the website willowcreek.org to see how you can get help.

- Mayo Clinic is a great tool to utilize if you would like to learn more about anxiety and depression.

- The National Alliance for Mental Illness is similar to TWLOHA in that it is an activist organization that offers support

- The American Psychological Association has many resources on its website such as journals and recently published articles on various mental illness-related topics.

Conclusion: I am Evergreen

I am like a flower.
I stand there, silent with my pretty colors as I am watered
and spoiled with the best type of soil.
I have a strong stem to help me bloom and blossom
with the rest of the beautiful flowers.
But when I have blossomed and my blooming is done,
what will become of me?
When I am cut from my roots and fresh soil,
will I still be happy?
Will I be put in a decorated glass filled with water for display?
So that someone can show me off
and take the credit of blooming such a beautiful flower,
credit that is not theirs?
Will I be sitting a room day and night, night and day
for other people to watch me like a mother watches her newborn?
Then what will become of me?
Will I rot, turn dark and shriveled?
Will I stay shriveled and dark until someone replaces me
with a flower that is more beautiful and radiant?
Then will I be tossed aside with the rest of the garbage
for no one to love and for no one to know me?
No, I will stand firm within my roots.
I will continue to grow and blossom.
When I grow old and shriveled, I will not be tossed aside.
I will stand until I can no longer.
For I am a still evergreen tree.
Through any weather I will stand and last forever.
I am not a flower.
I am not a flower.
I am a strong evergreen tree.
I am not envious of the beautiful flowers that surround me.
For in the horrible and stormy weather they will die,
But I will last forever.
I am not afraid of the children playing in the field.
I am not worried about them trampling over me
as guests that trample over welcome mats.
I am stronger and bigger than them and all of the balls that they will
throw at me
For I am evergreen, I will last forever.

ABOUT THE AUTHOR

Carmelita Booker studied general psychology at Eureka College, her alma mater. She is now studying industrial and organizational psychology at Adler University where she conducts student engagement meetings and researches the influences of online education and virtual university support on student success upon graduation. She also works as a freelance Senior Contributing Editor with Best Minds Associates with whom she develops curricula for metacognitive positive psychology courses. Dr. Gerard Meyer, CEO of BMA has stated that, "she is at the forefront of innovative concepts and techniques to hasten patient recovery and lasting happiness in life"… "she will become a star in our profession." Her other research interests include trauma psychology, neuropsychology, and forensic psychology. To learn more about Carmelita Booker, visit carmelitabooker.wordpress.com